Unlocking the Secrets of Selling Your Home:

Maximizing Value and Minimizing Stress

Silvina M Disla

Table of Contents

Introduction

Welcome to "Unlocking the Secrets of Selling Your Home," a comprehensive guide designed to empower home sellers with the knowledge and strategies needed to navigate the selling process successfully. Whether you're a first-time seller or a seasoned homeowner, selling your home can be a complex and challenging endeavor. From understanding the current real estate landscape to crafting an irresistible listing, negotiating like a pro, and closing the deal, this book covers every aspect of the selling process to help you achieve a successful sale.

In this book, I'll delve into the essential steps and strategies for selling your home effectively, from start to finish. I'll explore topics such as preparing your home for sale, pricing strategies that work, marketing your home effectively, negotiating like a pro, and handling post-sale considerations. Each chapter is packed with practical tips, expert insights, and valuable resources to guide you through the selling process and maximize the value of your home.

Throughout the book, I'll emphasize the importance of understanding market dynamics, setting realistic expectations, and leveraging effective strategies to attract potential buyers and achieve a successful sale. From enhancing curb appeal and decluttering your home to navigating multiple offers and closing the deal, I'll provide you with the tools and knowledge you need to succeed in today's competitive real estate market.

Whether you're looking to downsize, upgrade, or relocate, selling your home is a significant decision that requires careful planning and execution. With the guidance and resources provided in this book, you'll be well-equipped to navigate the selling process with confidence and achieve your goals as a home seller.

So let's dive in and unlock the secrets of selling your home. Whether you're looking to sell your home quickly or maximize its value, this book will provide you with the strategies and insights you need to achieve a successful sale. From preparing your home for sale to closing the deal, I'll walk you through each step of the process and empower you to succeed as a home seller.

About Silvina Disla

Silvina Disla is a dedicated and driven real estate agent with over two decades of full-time experience in the New Jersey and New York area. Being that Silvina recently moved to Miami, she is passionate in assisting people from out of state and other countries, into the Miami area, and making their transition seamless. As a full-time realtor, she has assisted a diverse clientele in finding their dream homes and making sound investment decisions. Her commitment to excellence and her in-depth knowledge of the local market trends have established her as a trusted and experienced professional in the industry. Silvina uses a personalized approach when dealing with buyers and sellers of diverse backgrounds, and she shines for her ability to think outside the box and for her "human touch" in everything she does. Silvina is also an artist (singer, recording artist and songwriter) taking pride and joy in her artistic nature, and being committed to her creative abilities in everything she does.

Experience:
Silvina Disla's extensive experience in real estate includes both residential and commercial. She has successfully negotiated and closed numerous transactions, ranging from first-time homebuyers to luxury properties and commercial investments. Her adaptability to changing market conditions and her local expertise make her a valuable asset to her clients.

Client-Centric Approach:
Silvina understands that buying or selling a property is a significant life event, and she is dedicated to making the process as smooth and stress-free as possible for her clients. She takes

the time to listen to their needs, answer their questions, and provide personalized guidance throughout the entire real estate journey.

Local Expertise:
Silvina Disla has a deep understanding of the local neighborhoods, schools, amenities, and market dynamics. She leverages this knowledge to help her clients make informed decisions that align with their lifestyle and investment goals.

Multilingual Advantage:
Silvina's ability to speak Spanish is a significant advantage in serving a diverse clientele. Her bilingual skills open doors to a wider range of opportunities, ensuring that clients who prefer Spanish-language support receive the same level of excellence in service.

Marketing Expertise:
Silvina employs cutting-edge marketing strategies to ensure her listings stand out in a competitive market. She uses professional photography, virtual tours, and social media promotion to showcase properties to their fullest potential. Her marketing skills help sellers achieve top dollar for their homes, and buyers to discover hidden gems.

Negotiation Skills:
One of Silvina Disla's key strengths is her negotiation skills. She has a proven track record of securing favorable deals for her clients. Her ability to navigate complex negotiations and advocate for her clients' best interests sets her apart in the industry.

Commitment to Excellence:
Silvina is committed to continuous learning and staying up-to-date with the latest industry trends and technologies. She holds

herself to the highest standards of professionalism and ethics, ensuring that her clients receive the best possible service.

Community Involvement:

Outside of her real estate career, Silvina Disla is an active member of the local community. She believes in giving back and is involved in various charitable organizations and community events. If you're looking for a dedicated, knowledgeable, and client-focused real estate agent who understands the Miami, New Jersey and New York area intimately and can assist in Spanish, contact Silvina Disla today. Whether you're buying, selling, or investing, Silvina is here to guide you every step of the way. Your real estate success is her top priority.

Chapter 1: Understanding the Steps

The sales process typically begins with an assessment of your property's value. This involves conducting a comparative market analysis (CMA) to determine a realistic listing price based on market trends, recent sales data, and the condition of your home.

Once you have determined the listing price, the next step is to prepare your home for sale. This may involve making repairs, decluttering, depersonalizing, and staging your home to showcase its best features and appeal to potential buyers. With your home ready for market, the next step is to create a comprehensive marketing plan to generate interest and attract buyers. This may include listing your property on multiple online platforms, hosting open houses, and utilizing social media and other marketing channels to reach a wide audience of potential buyers.

As inquiries and offers start to come in, you will need to negotiate with prospective buyers to secure the best possible deal. Negotiation is a critical part of the sales process, and it's essential to approach it with confidence and a clear understanding of your priorities and objectives.

Once you have accepted an offer, the final step is to close the deal. This involves completing any necessary paperwork, coordinating with the buyer's lender and title company, and ensuring a smooth and successful closing transaction.

Throughout the entire sales process, it's important to stay organized, communicate effectively with all parties involved, and be prepared to adapt to changing circumstances. By understanding the steps involved and having a clear plan in place, you can navigate the home selling process with confidence and achieve a successful outcome.

In the following chapters, we will delve deeper into each stage of the sales process, providing practical tips and advice to help you maximize your property sale and achieve your goals. Whether you're a first-time seller or a seasoned homeowner, this book will equip you with the knowledge and tools you need to succeed in today's competitive real estate market.

Chapter 2: Understanding the Market Dynamics

In this chapter, I'll delve into the essential aspects of understanding the market dynamics when selling your home. Whether you're a first-time seller or a seasoned homeowner, grasping the current real estate landscape and market trends is crucial for making informed decisions and achieving a successful sale.

The Current Real Estate Landscape

Before putting your home on the market, it's essential to familiarize yourself with the broader real estate landscape. The real estate market is influenced by various factors, including economic conditions, interest rates, housing supply and demand, and local market dynamics.

For instance, a strong economy and low unemployment rates generally correlate with a robust housing market, leading to increased buyer demand. Conversely, economic downturns may result in decreased demand and longer listing times. Additionally, factors such as population growth, job opportunities, and infrastructure developments can impact local housing markets differently.

Market Trends and Analysis

Staying abreast of market trends and conducting thorough market analysis is essential for setting realistic expectations and determining the optimal time to sell your home. Real estate professionals often use comparative market analysis (CMA) to evaluate recent sales of similar properties in your area, assessing factors such as sale prices, square footage, and property features.

Analyzing market trends involves examining key indicators such as median home prices, average days on market, and inventory levels. Tracking these metrics over time can provide valuable insights into whether the market favors buyers or sellers and help you strategize accordingly.

Setting Realistic Expectations

One of the most critical aspects of selling your home is setting realistic expectations. While every seller hopes to achieve a quick and profitable sale, it's essential to recognize that various factors influence the outcome, including market conditions, property condition, pricing strategy, and marketing efforts.

Consulting with a reputable real estate agent can help you gain a realistic understanding of your home's market value and the expected timeline for selling. Agents can provide valuable insights into local market trends, pricing strategies, and effective marketing techniques tailored to your specific property.

By understanding the current real estate landscape, analyzing market trends, and setting realistic expectations, you'll be better equipped to navigate the selling process successfully. In the next chapters, I'll delve deeper into preparing your home for sale, pricing strategies, and effective marketing techniques to maximize the value of your home and achieve a successful sale.

Chapter 3: Preparing Your Home for Sale

In this chapter, I'll explore the crucial steps involved in preparing your home for sale. From enhancing curb appeal to decluttering and making necessary repairs. Thorough preparation is essential for making a lasting impression on potential buyers and maximizing your home's value. Firstly, I'll refer to these main points below. Afterwards, I'll provide you with an indispensable, numbered list of tips that will help you stage your home and totally transform any property showing, ultimately creating a visually compelling presentation that will leave a lasting impression.

Enhancing Curb Appeal

First impressions matter, especially in real estate. Enhancing your home's curb appeal is vital for attracting potential buyers and creating a positive initial impression. Simple yet effective improvements such as mowing the lawn, trimming bushes, and planting flowers can significantly enhance the overall appearance of your property.

Consider investing in exterior upgrades such as repainting the front door, updating light fixtures, and power washing the exterior walls to give your home a fresh and inviting look. Address any visible maintenance issues such as cracked driveways, loose shingles, or chipped paint to ensure your home presents well from the curb.

Decluttering and Depersonalizing

When preparing your home for sale, decluttering and depersonalizing are key steps in creating a neutral and inviting environment for potential buyers. Start by removing excess clutter and personal items such as family photos, knick-knacks, and excessive furniture to create a sense of space and allow buyers to envision themselves living in the home.

Consider renting a storage unit to temporarily store bulky furniture or items that you don't use regularly. This will not only declutter your space but also make it easier for buyers to navigate through your home during showings.

Depersonalizing your home involves neutralizing decor and design elements to appeal to a broad range of potential buyers. Paint walls in neutral tones, remove bold wallpaper or paint colors, and replace personalized artwork with more universally appealing decor.

Repairs and Upgrades That Matter

Addressing necessary repairs and making strategic upgrades can significantly impact your home's perceived value and marketability. Start by conducting a thorough inspection of your home to identify any maintenance issues or areas in need of repair.

Focus on addressing visible defects such as leaky faucets, squeaky doors, and chipped paint, as well as more substantial issues like roof leaks, plumbing problems, or HVAC malfunctions. Investing in necessary repairs upfront can help prevent potential issues during the inspection process and instill confidence in potential buyers.

Strategic upgrades can also enhance your home's appeal and value. Focus on high-impact areas such as the kitchen and bathrooms, where minor updates like replacing outdated fixtures, refinishing cabinets, or updating countertops can make a significant difference.

Crafting an Irresistible Visual Presentation through Strategic Home Staging

1. Create a Welcoming Entryway: The entryway sets the tone for the rest of the home, so it's essential to make a good first impression. Consider adding a fresh coat of paint to the front door, updating

hardware, and adding tasteful decor to create a welcoming entryway that invites buyers in.

2. <u>Highlight Key Features:</u> Identify and highlight the key features of your home that are likely to appeal to potential buyers. Whether it's a fireplace, architectural details, or a stunning view, accentuate these features through strategic staging to draw attention and create interest.

3. <u>Use Neutral Colors and Decor:</u> Neutral colors and decor help create a cohesive and harmonious look that appeals to a wide range of buyers. Opt for neutral paint colors, furniture, and decor accents to create a blank canvas that allows potential buyers to visualize themselves living in the space.

4. <u>Maximize Natural Light:</u> Natural light enhances the overall appeal of a home and makes it feel bright, airy, and welcoming. Maximize natural light by opening curtains and blinds, trimming trees and bushes that block windows, and adding mirrors to reflect light and create the illusion of more space.

5. <u>Arrange Furniture Strategically:</u> Arrange furniture in a way that maximizes flow and functionality while highlighting the best features of each room. Create conversational seating areas, define focal points, and ensure that traffic flows smoothly throughout the space.

6. <u>Appeal to the Senses:</u> Appeal to potential buyers' senses by incorporating pleasant scents, soft music, and tactile textures throughout the home. Consider baking cookies before a showing,

playing soft background music, and adding plush throw pillows and blankets to create a cozy and inviting atmosphere.

7. Pay Attention to Details: Pay attention to the small details that can make a big difference in the overall presentation of your home. Replace outdated light fixtures, update cabinet hardware, and add fresh flowers or plants to add warmth and personality to the space.

By following all of these helpful insights, you'll create a compelling first impression to potential buyers and maximize your home's marketability. In the next chapters, I'll explore pricing strategies, crafting an irresistible listing, and effective marketing techniques to attract potential buyers and achieve a successful sale.

Chapter 4: Common Mistakes to Avoid Throughout the Selling Process

Selling a home can be a complex and challenging process, and even the most experienced sellers can make mistakes along the way. In this chapter, we'll explore some of the most common pitfalls to avoid throughout the selling process, empowering you to navigate the journey with confidence and avoid costly errors.

1. Overpricing Your Home:
One of the most common mistakes sellers make is overpricing their home. While it's natural to want to get the highest possible price for your property, pricing it too high can deter buyers and lead to your home sitting on the market for longer than necessary. Work with your real estate agent to set a realistic listing price based on market conditions and comparable sales.

2. Neglecting Repairs and Maintenance:
Buyers are typically looking for homes that are move-in ready, so it's important to address any necessary repairs and maintenance tasks before listing your property. Neglecting to make these repairs can turn off potential buyers and lead to lower offers.

3. Failing to Stage Your Home:
Home staging is a critical part of the selling process, as it helps buyers envision themselves living in your home. Failing to stage your home properly can make it appear less appealing and lead to lower offers. Take the time to declutter, depersonalize, and stage each room of your home to showcase its best features.

4. Ignoring Feedback from Potential Buyers:
When you receive feedback from potential buyers or their agents after a showing, it's important to take it seriously. Ignoring feedback or dismissing it outright can prevent you from making necessary adjustments to your marketing strategy or presentation, potentially costing you offers.

5. Being Unprepared for Negotiations:

Negotiation is a critical part of the selling process, and being unprepared can cost you money. Take the time to educate yourself about the negotiation process and work with your real estate agent to develop a strategy. Be prepared to advocate for your interests and be willing to compromise when necessary.

6. Not Considering All Offers:

While it's natural to be tempted to accept the first offer that comes along, it's important to consider all offers carefully. A lower offer may be more attractive if it comes with fewer contingencies or a quicker closing timeline. Work with your real estate agent to evaluate each offer and determine which one is best for you.

7. Skipping the Pre-Listing Inspection:

A pre-listing inspection can uncover any potential issues with your home before you put it on the market, allowing you to address them proactively. Skipping this step can lead to unpleasant surprises during the inspection period and potentially derail the sale.

By avoiding these common mistakes, you can increase your chances of a successful and profitable home sale. In the next chapter, we'll explore marketing techniques employed by top agents, so you can attract more buyers and generate higher offers for your property.

Chapter 5: Pricing Strategies That Work

In this chapter, I'll dive into the essential aspects of pricing your home strategically to attract potential buyers and maximize its market value. From understanding the importance of accurate pricing to navigating multiple offers, I'll explore effective pricing strategies that can help you achieve a successful sale.

The Importance of Accurate Pricing

Pricing your home accurately is one of the most critical factors in achieving a successful sale. Pricing too high can deter potential buyers and lead to extended listing times, while pricing too low may result in leaving money on the table. A comprehensive understanding of your home's market value and pricing trends is essential for determining the optimal listing price.

Real estate professionals often conduct comparative market analysis (CMA) to assess recent sales of similar properties in your area and determine a competitive listing price. Factors such as location, property size, condition, and amenities are taken into account when evaluating comparable properties and determining your home's market value.

Pricing Your Home Competitively

Competitive pricing involves setting a listing price that is in line with current market conditions and comparable properties in your area. Pricing your home competitively can attract more potential buyers, generate greater interest, and ultimately lead to a faster sale.

Consideration should be given to both the current market conditions and the unique features and amenities of your home when determining the listing price. While it's essential to aim for a competitive price, it's also crucial to leave room for negotiation and potential buyer incentives to ensure flexibility during the negotiation process.

Strategies for Handling Multiple Offers

In a competitive market, multiple offers on a property are not uncommon. Handling multiple offers requires careful consideration and strategic decision-making to maximize your home's sale price while ensuring a smooth and fair transaction process.

When faced with multiple offers, carefully review each offer's terms, including the purchase price, contingencies, financing terms, and proposed closing timeline. Consider factors such as the buyer's financial qualifications, earnest money deposit, and willingness to waive contingencies when evaluating offers.

In some cases, sellers may choose to counter multiple offers simultaneously or request a "best and final" offer from all interested buyers to facilitate a transparent and competitive bidding process. Working closely with your real estate agent to assess each offer's strengths and weaknesses can help you make informed decisions and negotiate effectively.

By understanding the importance of accurate pricing, pricing your home competitively, and navigating multiple offers strategically, you'll be better equipped to attract potential buyers and maximize your home's market value. In the next chapters, I'll explore crafting an irresistible listing, marketing your home effectively, and negotiating like a pro to achieve a successful sale.

Chapter 6: Crafting an Irresistible Listing

In this chapter, I'll explore the essential elements of crafting an irresistible listing that captures the attention of potential buyers and highlights the unique features and benefits of your home. From captivating photography and descriptions to leveraging technology for maximum exposure, I'll delve into effective strategies for creating a compelling listing that drives interest and generates offers.

Captivating Photography and Descriptions

The first step in creating an irresistible listing is capturing high-quality photography that showcases your home's best features and highlights its unique selling points. Professional real estate photography can make a significant difference in attracting potential buyers and enticing them to schedule a viewing.

When photographing your home, focus on capturing clear, well-lit images of each room from multiple angles. Highlight key features such as natural light, architectural details, and updated fixtures to showcase your home in its best light. Consider hiring a professional photographer with experience in real estate photography to ensure high-quality images that capture the essence of your home.

Accompanying your photographs with compelling descriptions is equally important in crafting an irresistible listing. Use descriptive language to paint a picture of life in your home, highlighting its unique features, amenities, and selling points. Focus on describing the benefits of each space rather than listing its features, and emphasize key selling points such as open floor plans, updated kitchens, or outdoor living spaces.

Leveraging Technology for Maximum Exposure

In today's digital age, leveraging technology is essential for maximizing the exposure of your listing and reaching potential buyers where they spend their time. Utilize online listing platforms, social media channels, and real estate websites to showcase your home to a broad audience of potential buyers.

Consider creating a virtual tour or video walkthrough of your home to provide potential buyers with an immersive experience and showcase its layout and features. Virtual tours allow buyers to explore your home remotely, providing them with a comprehensive view of the property and helping them envision themselves living there.

In addition to traditional listing platforms, consider leveraging social media channels such as Facebook, Instagram, and YouTube to promote your listing to a wider audience. Share high-quality images and videos of your home, along with compelling descriptions and highlights, to attract potential buyers and generate interest.

Highlighting Unique Selling Points

Highlighting the unique selling points of your home is crucial for differentiating it from other listings on the market and capturing the attention of potential buyers. Identify what sets your home apart from others in your area, whether it's its location, architectural style, or specific features and amenities.

Consider creating a list of key selling points to include in your listing description, such as recently renovated kitchens, energy-efficient upgrades, or outdoor living spaces. Emphasize the benefits of these features and how they enhance the overall living experience for potential buyers.

By crafting an irresistible listing with captivating photography and descriptions, leveraging technology for maximum exposure, and highlighting your home's unique selling points, you'll attract potential buyers and generate interest in your property. In the next chapters, I'll explore marketing your home effectively, negotiating like a pro, and closing the deal to achieve a successful sale.

Chapter 7: Marketing Your Home Effectively

In this chapter, I'll explore the essential strategies for marketing your home effectively to attract potential buyers and generate interest in your property. From leveraging traditional and digital channels to engaging with potential buyers and hosting open houses, I'll delve into effective marketing techniques that can help you achieve a successful sale.

Leveraging Traditional and Digital Channels

Effective marketing involves leveraging a combination of traditional and digital channels to reach potential buyers and showcase your home to a broad audience. Traditional marketing tactics such as yard signs, flyers, and direct mail can help generate local interest and attract potential buyers in your area.

In addition to traditional channels, digital marketing has become increasingly important in today's digital age. Utilize online listing platforms, real estate websites, and social media channels to showcase your home to a wider audience of potential buyers. Consider creating a dedicated website or landing page for your property, featuring high-quality images, virtual tours, and detailed descriptions to provide potential buyers with a comprehensive view of your home.

Engaging with Potential Buyers

Engaging with potential buyers is an essential aspect of effective marketing. Respond promptly to inquiries, schedule showings promptly, and provide detailed information about your home to interested buyers. Consider hosting open houses and private showings to allow potential buyers to explore your home and ask questions in person.

During showings, highlight key features and amenities of your home, and be prepared to answer questions about the property, neighborhood, and local amenities. Creating a welcoming and inviting atmosphere can help potential buyers envision themselves living in your home and increase their interest in making an offer.

Hosting Open Houses and Private Showings

Hosting open houses and private showings is an effective way to showcase your home to potential buyers and generate interest in your property. When hosting open houses, consider staging your home to highlight its best features and create an inviting atmosphere for potential buyers.

Promote your open house through traditional and digital channels, including yard signs, flyers, online listing platforms, and social media channels. Consider offering incentives such as refreshments or promotional materials to attract potential buyers and encourage them to attend your open house.

During private showings, focus on providing personalized attention to potential buyers and highlighting the unique features and benefits of your home. Be prepared to answer questions, address concerns, and provide additional information about the property to help potential buyers make an informed decision.

By leveraging traditional and digital channels, engaging with potential buyers, and hosting open houses and private showings, you'll effectively market your home and attract potential buyers to generate interest in your property. In the next chapters, I'll explore negotiating like a pro, closing the deal, and post-sale considerations to achieve a successful sale.

Chapter 8: Negotiating Like a Pro

In this chapter, I'll explore the art of negotiating like a pro when selling your home. Negotiation is a crucial aspect of the selling process, and mastering effective negotiation tactics can help you maximize your home's sale price and navigate the transaction process with confidence.

Understanding Buyer Psychology

Effective negotiation begins with understanding buyer psychology and motivations. Buyers may have various priorities and preferences when purchasing a home, including price, location, condition, and timing. By understanding what matters most to potential buyers, you can tailor your negotiation strategy to address their needs and preferences effectively.

Consideration should also be given to market conditions and buyer behavior. In a seller's market, where demand exceeds supply, sellers may have more leverage in negotiations. Conversely, in a buyer's market, where inventory levels are higher, buyers may have more negotiating power.

Counteroffers and Negotiation Tactics

When presented with an offer, it's essential to carefully review the terms and consider your goals and priorities. While price is a crucial factor, other terms such as contingencies, financing, and closing timeline should also be taken into account.

If the initial offer does not meet your expectations, consider making a counteroffer to negotiate more favorable terms. When making a counteroffer, be strategic in your approach and focus on achieving a win-win outcome for both parties. Avoid being overly aggressive or dismissive, as this can deter potential buyers and stall negotiations.

Negotiation tactics such as bundling concessions, offering incentives, and prioritizing certain terms can help bridge the gap between buyer and seller expectations. Working closely with a real estate agent, such as myself, to develop a negotiation strategy based on market conditions and buyer feedback can increase your chances of reaching a mutually beneficial agreement.

Navigating Inspection Requests

Inspections are a standard part of the homebuying process and can often lead to negotiation during the transaction. Buyers may request repairs or concessions based on the results of the inspection report, which can impact the final sale price and terms.

When navigating inspection requests, carefully review the inspection report and consider the significance of any identified issues. Focus on addressing safety hazards, structural concerns, and major mechanical issues that may affect the home's habitability or value.

Consider offering to make necessary repairs or provide credits to address significant issues identified during the inspection. Prioritize transparency and communication throughout the negotiation process to maintain goodwill and foster a positive relationship with the buyer.

Effective negotiation tactics, and navigating inspection requests strategically

1. Know Your Bottom Line: Before entering into negotiations, it's essential to know your bottom line—the minimum price you're willing to accept for your home. Understanding your financial goals and priorities allows you to negotiate confidently and avoid settling for less than you deserve.

2. <u>Gather Information:</u> Knowledge is power in negotiations. Gather information about recent comparable sales in your area, market trends, and the buyer's financial situation to inform your negotiation strategy and strengthen your position.

3. <u>Remain Emotionally Detached:</u> Negotiations can be emotional, but it's essential to remain calm, objective, and rational throughout the process. Emotions can cloud judgment and lead to poor decision-making, so focus on facts and logic to achieve your desired outcome.

4. <u>Be Flexible and Creative:</u> Flexibility is key to successful negotiations. Be open to alternative solutions and creative compromises that meet both parties' needs. By exploring different options, you increase the likelihood of reaching a mutually beneficial agreement.

5. <u>Prioritize Your Objectives:</u> Identify your priorities and objectives before entering negotiations. Whether it's a quick sale, a certain price threshold, or specific terms and conditions, knowing what matters most to you allows you to negotiate effectively and advocate for your interests.

6. <u>Use Leverage Wisely:</u> Identify and leverage your strengths and advantages in negotiations. Whether it's your home's desirable features, market demand, or multiple offers, use these factors to your advantage to negotiate from a position of strength.

7. <u>Practice Active Listening:</u> Effective negotiation involves active listening and understanding the other party's perspective. Pay attention to their concerns, interests, and priorities, and tailor your negotiation strategy accordingly to find common ground and reach a mutually satisfactory agreement.

8. <u>Know When to Walk Away:</u> Sometimes, the best negotiation tactic is knowing when to walk away. If the terms offered are not favorable or if the other party is unwilling to compromise, be prepared to walk away from the negotiation table and explore other options.

By understanding buyer psychology, employing effective negotiation tactics, and navigating inspection requests strategically, you'll negotiate like a pro and maximize your home's sale price. In the next chapters, I'll explore closing the deal, post-sale considerations, and avoiding common pitfalls to achieve a successful sale.

Chapter 9: Closing the Deal

In this chapter, I'll explore the final steps involved in closing the deal and completing the sale of your home. From working with title companies and attorneys to handling contingencies and legal requirements, I'll delve into the essential aspects of finalizing the sale and ensuring a smooth transaction process.

Working with Title Companies and Attorneys

Closing the deal involves coordinating with various parties, including title companies, attorneys, lenders, and other stakeholders. Title companies play a crucial role in facilitating the closing process by conducting a title search, verifying ownership of the property, and issuing title insurance to protect against any potential title defects.

Attorneys may also be involved in the closing process, especially in states where legal representation is required for real estate transactions. Attorneys can provide legal guidance, review contracts and closing documents, and ensure that all legal requirements are met throughout the transaction.

When selecting a title company or attorney, consider their experience, reputation, and track record of successful transactions. Work closely with your real estate agent to coordinate with these professionals and ensure a seamless closing process.

Handling Contingencies and Legal Requirements

Before the sale can be finalized, any contingencies outlined in the purchase agreement must be addressed, and all legal requirements must be met. Common contingencies include financing, appraisal, home inspection, and title review, among others.

If the buyer's financing is contingent on the sale of their current home or securing a mortgage, ensure that they meet their financing deadlines and provide necessary documentation to proceed with the transaction. Similarly, address any issues identified during the home inspection and negotiate repairs or credits as needed to satisfy the buyer's requirements.

Legal requirements vary by state and may include specific documentation, disclosures, and closing procedures mandated by local laws and regulations. Work closely with your real estate agent, title company, and attorney to ensure that all legal requirements are met and that the transaction proceeds smoothly.

Finalizing the Sale

Once all contingencies have been satisfied, and all legal requirements have been met, the sale can be finalized through a closing meeting or escrow process. During the closing, all parties involved in the transaction, including buyers, sellers, agents, and representatives from the title company or attorney's office, will review and sign the necessary closing documents.

At the closing, the buyer will typically provide the necessary funds to complete the purchase, including the down payment and closing costs. The title company or attorney will then facilitate the transfer of ownership and disbursement of funds, ensuring that all parties receive their respective payments and that the transaction is recorded appropriately.

By working with title companies and attorneys, handling contingencies and legal requirements, and finalizing the sale through a closing meeting or escrow process, you'll complete the sale of your home and ensure a smooth transaction process. In the next chapters, I'll explore post-sale considerations, avoiding common pitfalls, and expert insights and resources to empower you for success.

Chapter 10: Post-Sale Considerations

In this chapter, I'll explore the essential post-sale considerations that homeowners need to address after closing the deal on their home. From moving logistics and tips to handling tax implications and ensuring a smooth transition, I'll delve into the necessary steps to take after selling your home to ensure a successful transition.

Moving Logistics and Tips

After closing the deal on your home, the next step is to plan and execute your move to your new residence. Moving can be a complex and stressful process, but with careful planning and organization, you can make the transition smoother and more manageable.

Start by creating a moving timeline and checklist to outline the tasks you need to complete before, during, and after the move. This may include packing belongings, hiring movers or renting a moving truck, transferring utilities and services, and updating your address with relevant parties.

Consider decluttering and downsizing your belongings before the move to streamline the process and reduce moving costs. Donate or sell items you no longer need or use to lighten your load and simplify the moving process.

Handling Tax Implications

Selling your home can have tax implications that need to be addressed after closing the deal. Depending on your specific circumstances, you may be eligible for certain tax benefits or subject to capital gains taxes on the sale of your home.

Consult with a tax professional or financial advisor to understand the tax implications of selling your home and determine any potential tax liabilities or benefits. Factors such as the length of time you owned the property, the sale price, and any capital improvements made to the home may impact your tax obligations.

Consider exploring tax-saving strategies such as utilizing the home sale exclusion, which allows eligible homeowners to exclude up to a certain amount of capital gains from the sale of their primary residence. Understanding and planning for tax implications in advance can help you minimize tax liabilities and maximize your financial outcomes.

Ensuring a Smooth Transition

After selling your home, it's essential to ensure a smooth transition to your new residence and tie up any loose ends related to the sale. This may include canceling or transferring utilities, updating your address with relevant parties such as banks, insurance providers, and government agencies, and forwarding mail to your new address.

Consider conducting a final walkthrough of your home before closing to ensure that all agreed-upon repairs and maintenance items have been completed satisfactorily. This will help avoid any last-minute issues or surprises and ensure a seamless transition for both you and the buyer.

By addressing moving logistics and tips, handling tax implications, and ensuring a smooth transition to your new residence, you'll complete the post-sale process successfully and embark on your next chapter with confidence. In the next chapters, I'll explore avoiding common pitfalls, expert insights, and additional resources to empower you for success.

Chapter 11: Avoiding Common Pitfalls

In this chapter, I'll explore common pitfalls that home sellers often encounter during the selling process and provide strategies to avoid them. From identifying red flags in offers to managing emotional attachments, I'll delve into practical tips and advice to help you navigate the selling process successfully and achieve a smooth transaction.

Identifying Red Flags in Offers

When selling your home, it's essential to carefully review and evaluate offers from potential buyers to identify any red flags or potential issues. While receiving multiple offers can be exciting, it's crucial to scrutinize each offer and consider factors such as the buyer's financial qualifications, proposed terms, and contingencies.

Be cautious of offers that include vague or unrealistic terms, such as excessively low purchase prices, contingent upon the sale of the buyer's current home, or subject to financing with minimal earnest money deposits. Additionally, be wary of buyers who request excessive concessions or contingencies that may prolong the transaction process or increase your risk as a seller.

Work closely with your real estate agent to review and assess each offer's strengths and weaknesses, and consider seeking guidance from legal or financial professionals if needed. By identifying and addressing red flags in offers early in the process, you can mitigate risks and protect your interests throughout the transaction.

Dealing with Financing Issues

Financing issues are a common pitfall that home sellers may encounter during the selling process. Buyers may encounter challenges securing financing due to issues such as poor credit, insufficient income, or changes in lending requirements.

To avoid potential financing issues, work closely with your real estate agent to pre-screen potential buyers and prioritize offers from buyers with strong financial qualifications. Encourage buyers to obtain pre-approval or pre-qualification from a reputable lender before submitting an offer to ensure they have the financial means to purchase your home.

If financing issues arise during the transaction process, consider working with the buyer to explore alternative financing options or negotiate mutually acceptable solutions. Be prepared to be flexible and patient, and maintain open communication with all parties involved to facilitate a successful resolution.

Managing Emotional Attachments

One common pitfall that home sellers often encounter is managing emotional attachments to their home. Selling a home can evoke feelings of nostalgia, sentimental attachment, and reluctance to let go of cherished memories associated with the property.

To avoid letting emotional attachments interfere with the selling process, focus on the practical aspects of selling your home and the opportunities that lie ahead in your next chapter. Remind yourself of your reasons for selling and the goals you hope to achieve by moving forward with the sale.

Consider creating a farewell ritual or ceremony to say goodbye to your home and honor the memories you've shared there. Take photographs, write a letter to the new owners, or host a gathering with friends and family to commemorate the occasion and celebrate the next chapter in your life.

By identifying red flags in offers, dealing with financing issues proactively, and managing emotional attachments, you can navigate the selling process successfully and achieve a smooth transaction. In the next section, I'll conclude our exploration with expert insights and additional resources to empower you for success.

Chapter 12: Expert Insights and Resources

In this final chapter, I'll conclude my exploration of the selling process by providing expert insights and additional resources to empower you for success. From interviews with real estate professionals to helpful resources for home sellers, I'll provide valuable guidance and support as you embark on your journey to sell your home.

Interviews with Real Estate Professionals

To offer valuable insights and perspectives from real estate professionals, we've conducted interviews with experienced agents, brokers, and industry experts. These interviews provide valuable insights into the current real estate market, effective selling strategies, and tips for maximizing the value of your home.

Real estate professionals share their expertise on various topics, including pricing strategies, marketing techniques, negotiation tactics, and post-sale considerations. Their insights offer valuable guidance and practical advice to help you navigate the selling process successfully and achieve your goals as a home seller.

Additional Resources for Home Sellers

In addition to expert insights, we've compiled a list of additional resources and tools to support you throughout the selling process. These resources include:

1. Real Estate Websites: Explore reputable real estate websites and online listing platforms to research market trends, view comparable listings, and gather information on local housing market conditions.

2. Home Valuation Tools: Use online home valuation tools and calculators to estimate the current market value of your home based on recent sales data and market trends.

3. **Real Estate Agents:** Consult with experienced real estate agents who can provide personalized guidance and support throughout the selling process. A skilled agent can offer valuable insights, assist with pricing your home competitively, and navigate negotiations with potential buyers.

4. Legal and Financial Advisors: Seek guidance from legal and financial professionals, such as real estate attorneys and tax advisors, to ensure that you understand the legal and financial implications of selling your home and to protect your interests throughout the transaction.

5. Moving Services: Research reputable moving companies and services to assist with packing, transportation, and logistics during your move to your new residence.

6. Home Staging Services: Consider hiring professional home staging services to enhance the presentation of your home and make it more appealing to potential buyers.

7. Home Improvement Contractors: If necessary, enlist the services of reputable home improvement contractors to address any necessary repairs or upgrades to your home before listing it for sale.

By utilizing these additional resources and tools, you can navigate the selling process with confidence and maximize the value of your home. Whether you're a first-time seller or a seasoned homeowner, these resources provide valuable support and guidance to help you achieve a successful sale.

Looking to secure the highest possible price for your home?

There are numerous strategies you can employ to ensure your property fetches top dollar. Implementing these strategies can lead to a higher sales price. However, overlooking any of these crucial elements could result in settling for a lower price than you deserve.
That's why I'm offering a complimentary "Sell for Top Dollar" Consultation.

During this session, I will personally assess your home, providing insights into what steps need to be taken to achieve maximum value. I will offer guidance on marketing tactics, photography, pricing strategies, staging, negotiation techniques, and more. Each of these aspects plays a pivotal role in the success of your sale. By addressing them all effectively, you increase the likelihood of selling for top dollar. Conversely, neglecting even one of these elements could mean missing out on the price you rightfully deserve.

Conclusion: Empowering You for Success

As I conclude our journey through "Unlocking the Secrets of Selling Your Home," I hope that the insights, strategies, and resources provided in this book have empowered you with the knowledge and confidence to navigate the selling process successfully.

Selling your home can be a complex and challenging endeavor, but with careful planning, strategic decision-making, and the support of an experienced professional like myself, you can achieve your goals and maximize the value of your home.

Remember to stay informed, be proactive, and remain flexible throughout the process. By leveraging the insights and resources provided in this book, you'll be well-equipped to navigate the selling process with confidence and achieve a successful sale.

To schedule your Free, No Obligation "Sell for Top Dollar" Consultation, please contact me at 201-334-7703. We can arrange a convenient time to meet that works for both of us.
I eagerly anticipate the opportunity to assist you in achieving your selling goals!

Thank you for joining me on this journey, and I wish you the best of luck as you embark on your home selling journey. May your next chapter be filled with excitement, opportunity, and success!

- Silvina Disla, Licensed Real Estate Agent in both Florida & New Jersey
- Global Real Estate Advisor
- SilvinaDisla.Onesothebysrealty.com
- sdisla@onesothebysrealty.com
- 201-334-7703

www.ingramcontent.com/pod-product-compliance
Lightning Source LLC
Chambersburg PA
CBHW070453290526
45791CB00005B/2124